THE HISTORY OF PET DOGS

by Alicia Z. Klepeis

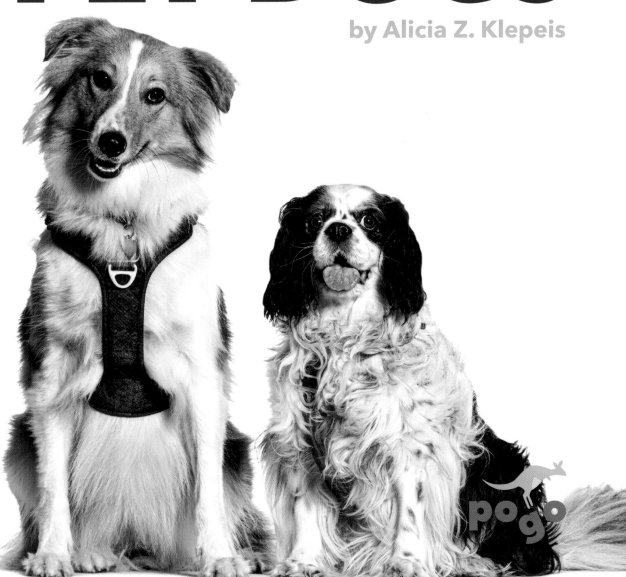

Ideas for Parents and Teachers

Pogo Books let children practice reading informational text while introducing them to nonfiction features such as headings, labels, sidebars, maps, and diagrams, as well as a table of contents, glossary, and index.

Carefully leveled text with a strong photo match offers early fluent readers the support they need to succeed.

Before Reading

- "Walk" through the book and point out the various nonfiction features. Ask the student what purpose each feature serves.
- Look at the glossary together. Read and discuss the words.

Read the Book

- Have the child read the book independently.
- Invite him or her to list questions that arise from reading.

After Reading

- Discuss the child's questions. Talk about how he or she might find answers to those questions.
- Prompt the child to think more. Ask: Do you have a pet dog or know someone who does? Do you think dogs make good pets? Why or why not?

Pogo Books are published by Jump!
5357 Penn Avenue South
Minneapolis, MN 55419
www.jumplibrary.com

Library of Congress Cataloging-in-Publication Data

Names: Klepeis, Alicia, 1971- author.
Title: The history of pet dogs / by Alicia Z. Klepeis.
Description: Minneapolis, MN: Jump!, Inc., 2024.
Series: History of pets | Includes index.
Audience: Ages 7-10
Identifiers: LCCN 2023000316 (print)
LCCN 2023000317 (ebook)
ISBN 9798885246101 (hardcover)
ISBN 9798885246118 (paperback)
ISBN 9798885246125 (ebook)
Subjects: LCSH: Dogs—Juvenile literature.
Classification: LCC SF426.5 .K64 2024 (print)
LCC SF426.5 (ebook)
DDC 636.7—dc23/eng/20230110
LC record available at https://lccn.loc.gov/2023000316
LC ebook record available at https://lccn.loc.gov/2023000317

Editor: Eliza Leahy
Designer: Molly Ballanger

Photo Credits: Ovchinnikova/Shutterstock, cover; GPPets/Shutterstock, 1; Erik Lam/Shutterstock, 3; Danielle Mussman/Dreamstime, 4; Nirinstar/Shutterstock, 5; koratmember/iStock, 6; Michal Martinek/Shutterstock, 7; Maria Ivanushkina/Shutterstock, 8-9; funboxphoto/Shutterstock, 10-11; kali9/iStock, 12; Nikonova Oli/Shutterstock, 13; LightField Studios/Shutterstock, 14-15; vyasphoto/Shutterstock, 16-17tl; Steve Oehlenschlager/Shutterstock, 16-17tr; fotografixx/iStock, 16-17bl; JG Photography/Alamy, 16-17br; Shaw Photography Co./Getty, 18-19; SolStock/iStock, 20-21; Eric Isselee/Shutterstock, 22tl, 22tr, 23; Jenson/Shutterstock, 22ml; Anna Aybetova/Shutterstock, 22mr; Jagodka/Shutterstock, 22bl; Kuznetsov Alexey/Shutterstock, 22br.

Printed in the United States of America at Corporate Graphics in North Mankato, Minnesota.

TABLE OF CONTENTS

CHAPTER 1

FUN WITH A FRIEND

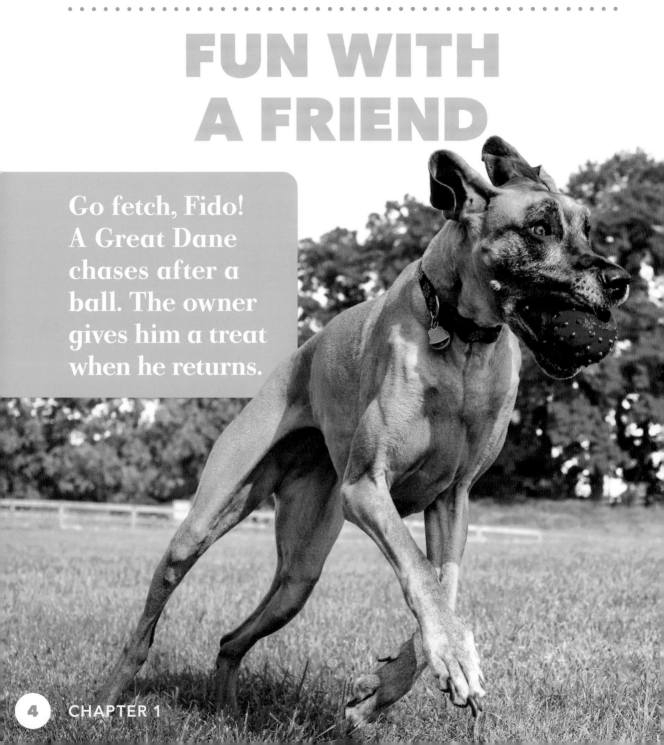

Go fetch, Fido! A Great Dane chases after a ball. The owner gives him a treat when he returns.

Today, dogs are beloved pets around the globe. But this wasn't always the case. How did these cute **canines** become such good friends to humans? Let's find out!

CHAPTER 2

FROM WOLF TO DOG

Dogs were the first animals **domesticated** by humans. Most experts believe it happened more than 20,000 years ago! How? People in **Eurasia** hunted and gathered their food. Wolves lived nearby.

wolf

Wolves likely ate meat humans left behind. Or people may have shared extra meat with the wolves. Either way, the wolves grew **tame**. They began hunting alongside humans.

Scientists study wolf **DNA** from long ago. They also look at **fossils**. Over time, wolves' bodies changed. Their skulls got smaller. So did their teeth and paws. They also became gentler. Today's pet dogs **descended** from these wolves!

TAKE A LOOK!

How is a wolf different from many dogs? Take a look!

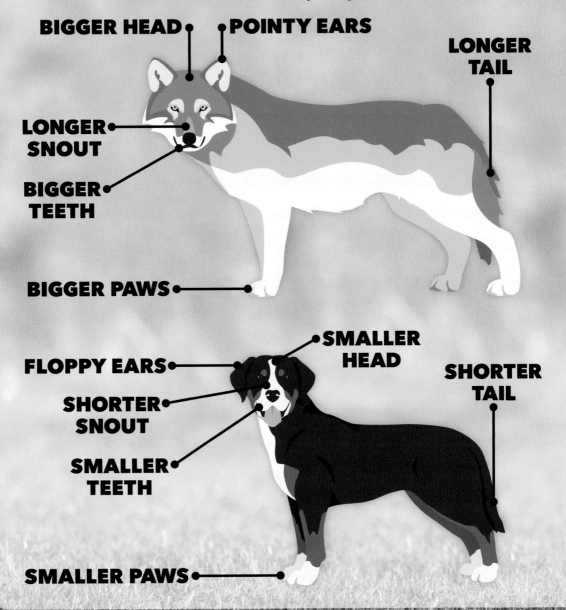

BIGGER HEAD   **POINTY EARS**

LONGER TAIL

LONGER SNOUT

BIGGER TEETH

BIGGER PAWS

SMALLER HEAD

FLOPPY EARS

SHORTER TAIL

SHORTER SNOUT

SMALLER TEETH

SMALLER PAWS

Ancient art shows dogs as pets. Roman **mosaics** and Egyptian paintings show dogs on leashes.

Over time, pet dogs spread around the globe. Scientists think they came with people to North America more than 10,000 years ago.

WHAT DO YOU THINK?

It is believed that a **land bridge** once connected North America and Asia. Dogs likely traveled across it. How else do you think dogs got to different parts of the world?

mosaic

CHAPTER 3

MOST POPULAR PET

Dogs are the most popular pet in the United States. Why? They are **loyal**, smart, and friendly. They are often our best friends! We **bond** with our pet dogs.

People in different times and places preferred different dog **breeds**. Some ancient Romans loved tiny dogs. So did European kings and queens. Some even built pockets into their clothing for them to sit in! Today, some people carry them in bags.

There are hundreds of dog breeds. In 2022, the most popular was the French bulldog. The Labrador retriever was most popular for 31 years before that. There are about 90 million pet dogs in the United States today. More than half of all households have one!

Labrador retriever

TAKE A LOOK!

In which states are people most likely to own a dog? Take a look!

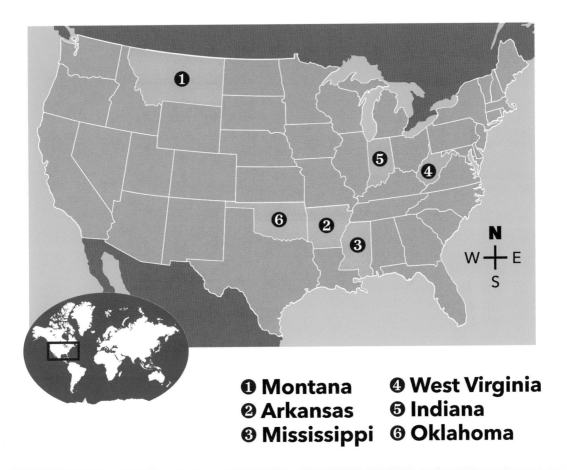

❶ **Montana**   ❹ **West Virginia**
❷ **Arkansas**   ❺ **Indiana**
❸ **Mississippi** ❻ **Oklahoma**

Many pet dogs in history have been working dogs. Some have served as guard or herding dogs. Others help hunt. Some help people with vision problems get around. Others work as **therapy** animals. It often takes one to two years to **train** these dogs.

WHAT DO YOU THINK?

Denver International Airport has more than 80 therapy dogs. They help calm nervous travelers. Do you think dogs make good therapy animals? Why or why not?

herding dog

hunting dog

service dog

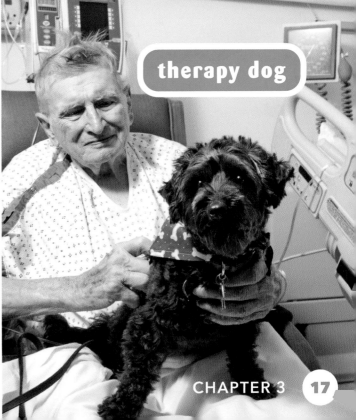

therapy dog

Many owners train their pet dogs.
Dogs can learn to sit and stay.
They learn to behave nicely
around other dogs and people.
Owners might use treats or
praise to reward them.

Playing or walking with a dog is good for both the pet and owner. Why? It gives them both exercise. People with pet dogs are less lonely. They can meet other dog owners at dog parks or other places. Would you like a pet dog?

DID YOU KNOW?

Nearly half of dogs in the United States sleep in bed with their owners.

QUICK FACTS & TOOLS

1. French bulldog

2. Labrador retriever

3. golden retriever

4. German shepherd

5. poodle

6. bulldog

ancient: Belonging to a period long ago.

bond: To form a close relationship with someone, such as a pet or family member.

breeds: Particular types of animals that are similar in most characteristics.

canines: Members of a group of animals that includes dogs, wolves, foxes, and jackals.

descended: Shared a common ancestor.

DNA: Molecules that carry our genes.

domesticated: Kept as pets.

Eurasia: The landmass which includes Europe and Asia.

fossils: Bones, shells, or traces of animals or plants from millions of years ago.

land bridge: A strip of land that connects two landmasses.

loyal: Faithful to a person.

mosaics: Pictures made up of small pieces of colored tile, stone, or glass.

tame: Taken from the wild and trained to live with or be useful to people.

therapy: Relating to treatment of mental or physical disorders.

train: To teach to perform a skill.

INDEX

TO LEARN MORE

Finding more information is as easy as 1, 2, 3.

❶ Go to www.factsurfer.com

❷ Enter "thehistoryofpetdogs" into the search box.

❸ Choose your book to see a list of websites.

FACT SURFER